The Art of the Presentation

How to Create and Deliver a Presentation that Gets Results

Gene,

Inspire them, Brother!

Lane Pierce Nov 2, 2019

By S. Lane Pierce

Published by:
The Foundation for Integrative Research
www.globalthought.org

Cover Design by S. Lane Pierce

ISBN: 978-1-7341057-0-4

About the Author

"Your path to success is knowledge of yourself."

S. Lane Pierce

S. Lane Pierce Lane is a Master Trainer of Neuro Linguistic Programming, Hypnosis, and other Technologies of the Mind. Lane is a Charter Member of the Advisory Board for the International Positive Psychological Association and is the founder of The Foundation for Integrative Research, Inc.

Lane has an extensive background in business and B2B sales. He is an accomplished presenter and specializes in training personnel in human factors and communication skills. He has helped businesses see growth, community organizations build strength, and his work in teaching how to control one's own mind has proven to change the lives of his clients in private practice as well.

He is devoted to his work of helping people to improve their lives. Lane shows the same deep compassion and commitment to his work, his community, and his family.

Dedication and Acknowledgements

First, I dedicate this book to Colleen. Where would I be without my lovely wife of more than twenty years? My love, we have seen a lot together. Thank you for always being on my side and supporting whatever I have endeavored to do. I love you.

Second, I dedicate this book to my children, Lori, Ben and Audra. You have helped shape me to be the man and father that I am. I love each of you and I am proud to be your Dad.

I want to acknowledge the following individuals; My dear friend and colleague, Dr. Yvonne Oswald, whose work in high-energy speech has contributed significantly to my skills as a communicator. My teacher and advisor, Robert "Silver" Baker who has on many occasions cajoled and prodded me to write a book and do many other things I have wanted to do. Aaron Bowley, my colleague, for his contributions. James Gibson and his wife Sam for their editorial review and contributions. And my many students who have simultaneously served as my teacher. Without them, I would not have learned as much as I have to this point.

Content

Prologue

One of the most rewarding experiences in life is the ability to stand before a group of any size and confidently deliver your thoughts, concerns, and solutions.

I remember when I was young in my career, and when I spoke to a group of people, it always felt as though I had to defend my words and thoughts. People would question me and challenge my position. Their posture and facial expressions seemed to always show that listening to me was tedious.

For myself, when I was 'in the hot seat' or stood in front of the group, I would begin to get really warm on the inside to the point I would begin to sweat on the outside. My mouth and tongue would become dry, and I would have to force words out of my throat. It was very uncomfortable, and I consciously knew there was no good reason for me to feel that way.

I knew that it was possible for me to be effective at delivering presentations because I saw others do it. I remember watching one of my colleagues, having been offered the opportunity to be the keynote speaker at a meeting with about 200 attendees from our customers and employees. He was funny. He was effective. The audience enjoyed his presentation... and he was promoted ahead of the rest of our team.

One thing I have noticed throughout my career is that those who are able to speak well and effectively communicate their ideas are able to get others to buy-in to their way of thinking. I also noticed that these were the same people who were getting promoted and earning more money.

I knew that I needed to change my attitude about my abilities and get some training in public speaking, so I began the process of learning how to improve my public speaking skills. This was a journey of years and I have learned much. In the process, I have become the teacher and have taught thousands how to maintain control over audiences, large and small, while teasing the attendees into embracing their ideas.

Imagine yourself now sharing your well-thought out comments while the audience nods approvingly. As you complete your presentation, they applaud and some even stand. Immediately after, a small line forms as a group of people approach you to offer their appreciation or ask for more detail.

I will tell you there is a certain sense of pride when others speak words of praise for your ability to sell an idea and entertain a group.

If it is possible for me, it is possible for you. I know this to be true.

You have picked up this book and are reading it for a reason. Perhaps someone who thinks highly of you offered this book as a gesture of his or her desire to be of service to you. Perhaps you gave yourself this gift. However you came by this material you must ask yourself;

- Do I want to communicate better at work?
- Do I want to be a master at selling my ideas, products, or services?
- Do I want to be able to get my opinions and ideas across to my friends and family?
- Do I want to have a higher level of influence in work, and family?
- Do I want to make more money?
- Do I want to be respected?
- Do I want more out of life?

Get ready. The content contained herein may well improve not only your presentation skills, but perhaps your life as well.

This book will reveal to you how the human mind works. When you have a clear understanding of that, it will begin to change how you engage with life until such time that you have created a new 'normal'. One where you are creating your life rather than responding to it.

Do not take any advice here at face value. I challenge you to prove these techniques for yourself.

Expect to learn something new. Expect to have revealed what you already know - but didn't know you know. Expect to enjoy the process.

So, let's get on with it shall we?

Preface

"Things do not happen, things are made to happen."

John Fitzgerald Kennedy

Getting the Most from This Experience

Perhaps the first and most important thing for you to consider to have the best possible learning from this book is an understanding of why you are reading it. What is it that you desire to learn? Is your focus on improving your sales? Do you want to be a better Manager, or Coach? Could your communication with your spouse or children improve? All of these are great uses for the knowledge you will learn within the following pages.

My intent is to share with you my personal experience of how to master your communication skills. To do that, I have written this book as though you and I are having a conversation. I have cut out the unnecessary dialog used to pad the length of a book to some editor's demand and I have preferred to keep the information clear and to the point. In doing so, I encourage you to ponder the lessons contained herein and look for the additional meaning between the words.

"I" and "me" refers to me, the author.

"You" refers to you.

"Him", "his", "them", "they", etc. refer to those who are listening to you. I would prefer to have made the book gender neutral and when I did, it seemed so clinical and unfriendly. I chose to be male-specific in my writing and to keep it consistent. I know that roughly half of my readers are women and I hope half of you will forgive me (and I think my female readers can make the mental-shifts easier).

"Audience" and "listener" refer to those who are receiving your presentation. "Audience" is generally used in reference to large groups. "Listener" is used to refer to a single person that you are engaging in your presentation even if they are in a large group.

"Presentation", "communication", and "content" are really the same. Your presentation is your communication and vice-versa.

The content of this book is not exhaustive. To do that would require a tome covering all the mental aspects of how people communicate and how they construct meaning and even reality itself. Certainly, that is more than what is needed for you to be an excellent communicator.

My objective is to write a 'how-to' book for you. I want to share with you the skills I have been effectively using in giving presentations.

I have over thirty-years of experience in giving presentations that range from training people in communication skills through presenting and selling high-end technology for large companies. I routinely get feedback that the presentation was among the best the audience has had. Other presenters say to me, "I am saying the same things you are. Why do I not get the results you are getting?" The answer to this is simple really; it is not what I am saying; rather, it is *how* I am saying it. That is the difference that makes a difference in my presentation.

I have taken the best content from my experience and distilled it down to its essential elements and I present these to you for your easy assimilation into what you are now doing.

The chapters are divided into logical blocks of information and are meant to build on each other. I recommend that you first read through this book in its entirety. Highlight things of interest. Indicate things you already know or practice and make notes on those you do not.

Having read the book once, take each chapter and begin to train yourself in these new skills. Like any learning process, honor yourself enough to put in some time and make the information conscious. Make a real effort each day to develop a skill and turn that skill into a habit. This is how you make real changes in your life and that is what this book is about now, isn't it?

Begin with **You: Chapter 1**. Now, get yourself prepared to be an excellent presenter and get yourself ready to learn more.

Remember, the key to your success is to put these techniques into practice. Some may seem awkward at first. Fine. Anytime you do something for the first time, there is a chance it could feel awkward. Make it a part of how you prepare and deliver your presentation and the awkwardness will be replaced with excellence.

I remember the first time I stood in front of a group of people to make a presentation and purposefully refrained from using my hands. It was a task to learn how to improve my physical presence and tone of voice to make a point. I stood there being very aware that my hands seemed to hang heavily at my side. Everything in my head told me this was unnatural and uncomfortable. After all, my hands always just seem to move on their own as an integral part of the act of communicating. It was extremely awkward, and I just *knew* the whole audience was participating in my discomfort.

I began to get into my presentation and as I forgot about my hands, they took on a life of the own and resumed their roll, flapping about at my side. My first presentation while impersonating a penguin! Eventually, the awkwardness falls away and competence take over. It is just a learning process. You can do this!

You: Chapter 1

Preparing Your Most Valuable Resource – You

"Nosce te ipsum (Know thy self)"

Ancient Greek Aphorism

Where is your head?

Whether or not you intend to do so, you are making one or, more likely, several presentations each day. If you are sharing your ideas, trying to get a raise, or trying to get a meeting, you are making a presentation. Pretty much anything other than ordering lunch is a presentation. What is it that you are presenting? You are presenting your perspective on the world and hoping that others will join you in your perspective. It is the reason *why* we communicate.

If you're always communicating and you're always presenting, then it makes sense to do it well, doesn't it?

From time long-established, those who were skilled in communication were often lauded as leaders. They may have been leaders of thought or leaders of business. Where you find an effective communicator, you find one who is capable of moving people into action. You will find a leader.

People are funny creatures and often quite predictable. While we might not be able to predict what a person will say or do, we can predict that they will DO something. An effective communicator can arouse the listener's interest, ignite their passion, and drive them to action to DO whatever is in alignment with the presenter's intentions. That, my friend, is selling.

Now before you get all twisted up about what I have written and say, "This sounds like manipulation!" Take a deep breath and let me explain... YOU'RE RIGHT! This is all about manipulation and influence. An effective communicator always wants to manipulate the thinking of the listener to the speaker's way of thinking. Every time you open your mouth you are attempting to manipulate someone to your way of thinking. Everybody is attempting to manipulate everybody else every day. It's what we do. If you have some negative charge on the idea of manipulating others, keep in mind that manipulation is not good or bad in itself. It's your heart and your ethics that make manipulation good or bad. Be effective in your use of manipulation for the good of others.

Before you can persuade anyone else, you have to get yourself right. What's in your head? What are the attitudes, beliefs, values, and thinking processes you are running in your head? I assure you that whatever is going on in there is what will eventually find its way out of your mouth and into the mind of your listener.

Perhaps you remember this day from your past? You woke up to the sound of your neighbor's barking dog. Your nerves were raw like they had been exposed to the elements all night. When you stepped out of bed, you stepped on the cat. The toothpaste squeezed out of the backend of the tube. Your toast burned. How did your tire get a flat just sitting in the driveway overnight?

Things happen, and no matter what, you still must be the superstar presenter. What you do now, before walking into your presentation, is let it go and be fully engaged in doing *your* presentation. Your task, being the excellent communicator that you are, is to let go the negative things that occurred in the past and tune your mind toward perfect execution in the now.

The professional actor has a saying, "The show must go on." Generally, this is true in your case too. Your presentation is your show. Anything less than your best performance is not acceptable, and your presentation must happen.

I have done presentations when feeling nauseated, I have done presentations after receiving bad news, and I have done presentations when I only had just an hour of sleep. One time I sat down and recorded 6 presentations after 16 hours of work, while in the midst of what the doctor told me later was West Nile Fever. I was exhausted! Because it was being recorded, it was even more important that I muster my personal resources and give it my best. Unless you know my voice, it is difficult to tell that I was really not well when making the recordings.

Now, it is true that sometimes it is not reasonable to go on with the presentation. If your child was admitted to the hospital for unknown reasons this morning, that is worthy of a 'no-show'. I know I do not need to provide examples here. You're a professional. You know when to call in and bow out.

Relax!

Your mind and your body are what make your presentation. Your mental and emotional states will project themselves into your presentation and this often is the difference between a great or not-so-great presentation. When you are relaxed, words come more easily, and your audience perceives confidence from you.

Stuff happens and you are not always in control of all the circumstances. When that occurs, it can create stress and stress is the killer of an otherwise excellent presentation.

You are about to learn one of the greatest secrets of how your mind and body work together in order to eliminate stress and replace it with calmness. Some people have a great fear of speaking in front of others and this is a surefire way to tame that fear.

Have you noticed that when you are in stress-mode, your field of vision narrows? The more stressed you become, the tighter and tunnel-like your field of vision becomes. In a like manner, when you are relaxed, your field of vision widens. This is a simple function of the body that often occurs out of your awareness. Stress will reduce or expand your field of vision. The secret is that this is a two-way street. If you want to relax, just become aware of what is in the periphery of your vision. Bingo! That's it. Your body will automatically begin to relax, and your mind will ease.

To activate your peripheral vision, find some spot out in front of you. Now, keeping your eyes on that spot, allow yourself to become aware of what is to the right and left of you. Next, become aware of what is above and below you. When you do this, you will notice a sense of calm accompanied by a sense of expanded visual acquity. I refer to this a 'softening your gaze' or 'peripheral vision'.

Soften your gaze to help calm your mind and relax your body. You will also find that this technique tends to help you speak more conversantly when giving your presentation.

14

States to Hold in Mind

Remember, what is in your head is what comes out in your communication. Your body, your tone of voice, and your words are all part of your communication. We'll dive deep into that later. The point is if you're feeling grumpy or unsure of yourself, you might as well tattoo it on your forehead. I guarantee your audiences will pick up on it. Worse, they will make assumptions about what is wrong with you and, if they are in a bad mood, they add that to what they see on your face and all the sudden, they think you're one-step away from being committed to the psych ward. For certain, they will not trust you and they will not believe you. Your presentation will fail.

A person who has been trained in telephone communications is taught to always sit up straight, hold their shoulders up and to smile when they talk. It makes a difference. It makes a difference to both the speaker and the listener. As the speaker, if you are sitting up straight with your shoulders up, chest out, chin up, eyes sharp and focused ahead, with a smile on your face... you can't get upset! Your physiology simply will not support it.

To give yourself an advantage in how your communication comes across to your listener, decide on what mental states or resources you should possess during your presentation. What is important to you, your values, often make great mental states for resourcefulness as a speaker. What values might you hold a speaker to that you respect; sincerity, confidence, knowledge, integrity, credibility, etc.? This list is the kind of attitudes and beliefs you will hold in your own mind during your presentations.

For me, the attitudes, beliefs, and states I hold in mind during a presentation are;

- Proud

  I have pride in myself, my company, my service, my product.

- Humble

  I am an expert and, I still have more to learn. You are my teacher even while I am being your expert.

- Courageous

  I am willing to do what it takes to be successful. I am willing to face any challenge be it technological or personal in order to be successful.

- Service

  I will serve you to our mutual benefit.

Now, you need to create your list. Think about a speaker or presenter whom you respect. This might include well-known speakers like Zig Ziglar or Tony Robbins. What is it about that person that connects you to them? What is it about them that creates credibility in your mind? Take a minute and consider the 4 or 5 values you perceive in your idea of a 'best speaker' and write your list below.

My Resources and Values

Of an Excellent Speaker / Presenter

How to get your act together

If you had a way to help you get your head right and put you into the best possible resourceful state and, you could do that anytime you desire, how much better will your presentations be?

I will tell you that this next step is a key element in being an excellent presenter. You may think it is odd but, I promise, it is totally worth it. Every speaker worth their salt has done this or does this intuitively.

Task #1 – Pick a theme song.

Every superhero has one, why not you? Even the bad guys have cool theme songs (think Darth Vader). Your theme song should embody the concepts of your values you listed above. It should evoke within you a kind of energy that makes you want to move into action. "Gonna Fly Now" (Theme from Rocky) composed by Bill Conti, “Flash” by Queen, or the theme song to Cool Hand Luke by Lalo Schifrin, these are all great choices and motivating songs. Pick a song that speaks to you.

If you have a large chunk of cash lying around, hire someone to write your theme song. If not, borrow one. My theme song? "I Have the Touch" by Peter Gabriel.

Professionals of all levels use this. I bet that you could walk into any gym with professional athletes and you will find several of them wearing headphones and listening to some motivational tunes. They might be lifting weights, or they might just be sitting quietly with their eyes closed but they are doing the same thing. They are using their songs to get their mind right.

Pick a great song. It will be with you for the rest of your life.

Task #2 – Associate your mental states with your theme song.

Have you noticed that when you recall some songs, they evoke particular memories and emotions in you? Perhaps a song that reminds you of prom night or a song that reminds you of when your team won against all odds ("We Are The Champions"). Next to smell, sound is highly evocative of memories and emotions.

Now that you have your theme song selected, it's time to associate your resources to your song so each time you hear your song, you will be amped up and ready.

For each resource you wrote previously, do the following. In this exercise, we'll presuppose the resource is 'pride'.

The Process

Step 1 Remember a specific time when you felt 'pride'. Remember a specific time where the feeling of pride was the strongest emotion present. Write down two or three words to remind yourself of the event.

Step 2 Play your theme song. I recommend using headphones so you get the full richness of the music.

Step 3 Close your eyes and as vividly as you can, recall that specific 'pride' event. Stay focused on this event and the successful outcome of the event. Remember what you saw, what you heard, and what you felt. Remember who was there, if anyone, and what they said or did as well. Really pretend you are there again.

Step 4 Rinse and repeat... do Steps 1 through 3 with each of your resources.

That's it. That is how you associate your resources to your theme song. The more vividly you can recall the event and the more strongly you can recreate the feeling in your mind, the better this process is. Really get into it. Go into a room by yourself. Kick everyone out of the house. Jump up and down. Do fist pumps. Look in the mirror and point at that magnificent reflection and shout, "*You frickin' ROCK!*" If you think this is silly, then my question for you is, "Do you want this? Do you really want it?"

The key here is to *FEEL* the emotion while hearing your theme song. I recommend you do this simple three-step process, three times with each of your resources. Use the same song each time. This is a fun process so make a decision to commit yourself to it.

Speaking Literally

Some speakers will speak literally. That is to say that everything that comes out of their mouth is exactly what they mean. There is no innuendo, no hidden agenda, nothing for you to guess. When they speak, you can rely on what you hear as though it is fact as they understand it.

When a literal speaker says, "I'm thirsty", they are in no way implying you need to do anything about it. They are simply stating the fact that they are indeed thirsty.

Some speakers will speak inferentially. Inferential speakers will imply, hint, or give clues as to what they desire without coming out and directly saying it. When an inferential speaker is talking, you have to make the extra effort to figure out what it is that they are saying. This can get wearisome on the listener (especially if the listener listens literally).

When an inferential speaker says, "I'm thirsty", they may be implying it would be nice for someone to offer them a drink.

As implied above, there are also literal listeners and inferential listeners. It helps to know your own Speaking Style and Listening Style, so I recommend you take some time to figure that out.

To determine your Listening Style ask yourself, “If someone I know quite well says that they are thirsty, would I feel compelled to do something about it?” If the answer is ‘yes’ then you are probably more of an inferential listener.

My Listening Style is: ______________________________

To determine your Speaking Style ask yourself how you would handle someone who is not performing as well as they should. Would you come to the point and tell them directly or would you imply and give them clues? If you would tell them directly, then you are more literal in your speaking.

My Speaking Style is: ______________________________

Inferential and literal styles are both useful for speaking and listening and you should strive to choose which style you use in certain situations. When giving your presentation, it is typical for you to use both. Remember, a literal speaker is easy for most people to listen to because the listener does not have to work at discovering the meaning in what the speaker is saying.

Be careful in your 'literal-ness' though. Be mindful of your audience. A literal speaker could easily offend an inferential listener. Remember whom you are talking to and take into account any cultural differences. In some cultures, maintaining 'face' is very important and, as a result, telling a person 'no' is something that is usually delivered inferentially.

Say it the way you want it

The next skill you want to develop is your focus. One of the great truths in life is that you will eventually get what you focus on. Well, if that is the case then doesn't it seem logical to focus on what you want rather than what you don't want?

When you are driving down the road, your focus is on the road ahead of you. What happens when you look at the car driving in the lane next to you on the right? Your car will begin to drift to the right. Right? Ask anyone you know who rides a motorcycle and they will tell you that the bike will go wherever you are focusing. If you focus on the ditch, you will end up in the ditch. If you focus on where you will exit the curve, then that is where you will be.

The same is true for life. If you focus on feeling bad, then you will feel bad. If you focus on feeling good, then you will feel better.

If you take only *one* thing from this book, take this lesson. What you focus on you will manage to create for yourself. ***Focus on what you want, every day.***

To understand why this is the case you need to understand how the unconscious mind works. The unconscious mind's job is to make meaning of everything. The unconscious mind has no role in 'understanding', that is the conscious mind's job. In order to give things meaning, the unconscious necessarily takes everything personally and quite literally.

One thing the unconscious cannot do is process a negation. Negatives, like 'not' or 'no', are logical Boolean functions and that is the domain of the rational conscious mind. The unconscious mind has no way to process these negations.

If I say, "Do NOT think of a purple dinosaur." What pops up in your head? The purple dinosaur of course... it must... there is no choice.

The unconscious mind is the domain of emotions and meaning-making. The conscious mind is the domain of rationalization. In order to process any communication, the two must work together and they carry on a dialog that goes something like this...

The ear sends in the message, "Do not think of a purple dinosaur."

The conscious mind says, "What the heck is this 'purple dinosaur' I am not supposed to think about?"

The unconscious mind responds with, "A *purple* dinosaur? Well let's see... I think it is something like this..." and it presents a picture of a purple dinosaur to the conscious mind.

Then the conscious mind tries to NOT think of the purple dinosaur, "Doh! I'm NOT supposed to think about that. Make me a green dinosaur instead."

Making Meaning

Let's take this notion of 'say it the way you want it' to the next level. When the unconscious mind processes language it does so strictly in the form of a picture and, we all know, a picture is worth a thousand words. When you hear the word 'mom', a picture pops up in your mind and along with it comes a whole host of data. The picture is likely of your mom or someone who you consider a mom. You may also get a sense of the sound of their voice, an emotional feeling of this person, and other bits of data around smell, touch, and so on.

Every word always carries some form of data and energy with it. The energy contained within the word is what we refer to when we talk about the *semantics* of the word. It is the semantics, along with the context that the word was used in, that determine our meaning of the word. What this says is that for every word you hear, you get a picture with data, and energy and, at some level, that energy will impact you in a subtle, unconscious way. Words with high-energy are more useful for a presenter than low-energy words because they leave the listener feeling better (even though the listener doesn't know why). For a more detailed study on this subject, I recommend reading *Every Word Has Power* by my dear friend, Dr. Yvonne Oswald, PhD. The examples below were adopted from her book.

Example of Low-Energy Dialog

Brian: "Good morning! How are you?"

Robert: "Not *bad.* I was pretty *sick* last weekend and I'm still trying to shake it off. I always get *sick* at this time of year. It gets me really *depressed.*"

Brian: "*Poor* you! *That sucks.* Did you get that flu that's going around? It's a *really nasty* one this time. Everyone's catching it – it seems to last for weeks because... you think it's gone and then it comes back. It's *hard* to get rid of. Anyway, I've got the book you ordered. *It's a bit expensive* – twenty-five dollars, I'm *afraid.*"

Robert: "Oh! *I'm broke right now* so, do you mind if I get the money to you after I get paid next week, or will a postdated check do?"

Brian: "Don't *worry.* I know *it's really hard right now. The economy is always down* this time of the year. Whatever works for you is fine."

Robert: "Thank you very much!"

Brian: "No *problem.* See you later."

If you check-in with yourself after reading that conversation you will notice that on some level, you feel less good. Now let's see how the same dialog might go using words that evoke better energy.

Example of High-Energy Dialog

Robert: "Good morning, Brian. Are you *well*?"

Brian: "Actually, I'm *much better*. I *was not feeling well* last weekend, so I've decided to *get fit and healthy* this summer and *maintain a good attitude*."

Robert: "*Great*! I wish you *success*. *I've got terrific news* for you; the book you ordered has arrived. It's twenty-five dollars."

Brian: "*Wonderful*! Can I collect it next week? I'll have *more money* then!"

Robert: "Sure! Whatever works for you is *fine*. I'll see you soon."

Brian: "*Thanks a million*!"

Robert: "It's my *pleasure*."

After reading the two examples above, I predict the second leaves you feeling a bit better than the first. It was chockfull of high-energy words. The pictures in your head along with the semantics of those high-energy words are what left you feeling good.

Now, let's go back to 'say it the way you want it' for a moment. You now recognize that 'problem' is a low energy word and, since the unconscious mind does not process a negation, 'no problem', though it is referring to a positive, still has a negative impact on the listener. Say it the way you want it... an appropriate response might be, "My pleasure."

Remain externally focused on the listener's needs/pains/desires.

Another hallmark of an excellent presenter is that each member of the audience feels as though they have made a personal connection with the speaker. A great presenter will capture you and bring you into his story. He will evoke emotions within you and engage your mind in a mutual creation of his reality. If you have ever attended a conference or even just a lunch meeting, when it seems as though the entire room disappears and there is only you and the speaker present, that's the environment an excellent presenter creates.

As an excellent presenter, it is your responsibility to make and maintain that connection with each individual member of your audience. You do this by establishing rapport and keeping the listener as your object of attention.

We'll cover rapport in great detail in Setup: Chapter 5.

The question now is this, how do you stay externally focused on the listener so that they feel they have that continual connection with you?

#1 Know your content

When presenting, you are running two mental processes; ethos (character) and logos (word), in order to create pathos (experience). The key to providing a great experience is to maintain these two mental processes so they jointly create the experience you want your audience to have.

Ethos is the character or reputation you use and communicate to your audience in order to make your content credible. How you dress, how you introduce yourself, the energy you bring to your presentation, and your word choices are all part of ethos. Ethos gives the audience a mental structure to hold your content. That structure also contributes to the listener's interpretation of the content. Much of ethos is unconscious and is therefore developed through habits and your personality. If your presentation is to be a high-energy presentation, then you should adopt attitudes and behaviors that communicate high-energy.

Logos is the content. It is the data, or information, you are communicating to your audience. Logos is the conscious component of your presentation. It is related to logic and details. The listener will place the logos content into the structure created by the ethos. This is how they extrapolate meaning and create their experience.

The most important thing you can do as an excellent presenter is to know your content, so much so that you can speak of it extemporaneously. If you are not solid with your content, you turn your mental attention inward in an attempt to dynamically create the content. This will be picked up and perceived by your audience in ways you cannot predict. They may perceive you are preoccupied and not interested in them or why they are there. Or they may perceive that you are not the expert they were expecting.

It is true that, from time to time, the audience likes to play "stump the presenter". You need to be ready for this too. You may want to pause, access your logos and create the content in order to answer the question or, you may want to defer or deflect the comment. Whatever you choose, there are specific skills around those techniques also. See the sections on 'What to do when you're dying on the platform' and 'Answering Questions'.

#2 Eyes up!

In order to help you stay externally focused, it helps to keep your eyes up, so you are looking out towards your audience. This helps build that one-on-one connection. It's not just about looking at your audience, look at each member of the audience. Make eye contact. Hold it for a few long seconds and move on.

If you have a large audience, it can get difficult to make eye contact with each one. Make eye contact with as many as you can and be sure you do with any leaders in the room. If there is someone present that other attendees look up to, make sure you have established good eye contact with that person.

When you have good eye contact, give a slight nod or some form of acknowledgment.

#3 Develop Your Conscious Use of Indirect Language

The 'meaning-making' process is a very personal task. Each person listening to your presentation (your words) will contrive meaning from those words in some way that is consistent with their values, beliefs, context, emotional state, and so on. That is to say that each person will construct their own meaning, or understanding, of your words from within themselves. You only have an indirect link to their understanding in the communication process. In order to be understood, you must engage the listener's mind to think the thoughts that are consistent with the meaning you want them to get.

The skill is Use of Indirect Language to induce the listener to think the thoughts you want them to think while they are doing so in a way that is consistent with their projection of reality. I know by now you may be thinking, 'What?' or 'How do I do that?'. That's okay. This is one of those things you are about to learn that you already do.

Regular human conversation is overflowing with Indirect Language. It *is* how we communicate. For example, I might ask you, “What did you have for lunch?” and you might respond, rather indirectly, “I had some pizza.” In order for me to understand what it was you ate, I must create my own interpretation of ‘pizza’ which might be; a single triangular slice of thin-crust pepperoni with cheese cooked just to where some of the cheese has browned and the edges of the pepperoni are slightly crisp. And perhaps the reality is that you had 3 square pieces of a cheese only pizza with a thin crust. So long as it is unnecessary to get into the details, you provided just enough information for me to derive my own meaning, and my understanding of what you ate for lunch is sufficient. The net effect is that, if I like my picture of pizza, I will have positive feelings about what you ate and that might evoke additional thoughts, topics of discussion, or even enhance the rapport we are experiencing. You spoke to me indirectly, even if it was only for the sake of efficiency.

The benefit in speaking indirectly is efficiency in communication, and when executed effectively, the listener gets and internal experience of *confidence* and *knowing*. These are critical components in influential communication and often the purpose or intent of a presentation.

Some Examples of Indirect Language

Presumed Thought (or Mind Reading) is where one implies they know something about what the other person is thinking but there is no direct link or understanding as to how they came to this knowledge. For example, "By now *you are thinking about* how this would benefit your current project." or even "These aren't the droids *you are looking for.*"

Unspecified Comparison is where a person offers a value judgement about something without specifying the thing they are comparing it to. A favorite example of mine comes from the Dilbert comic strip by Scott Adams. The pointy-haired boss says to Dilbert, "Why did this take so long?" To which Dilbert replies, "You're comparing a task – the likes of which has never been done – to your imagination of how long such things should take." And the pointy-haired boss says, "Well then, the quality is bad." And Dilbert says, "Compared to...?"

Implied Outcomes is where the acceptance of one idea implies the outcome or the next idea. For example, "*Because* you are reading this book, *that means* you are learning." And, "With a simple application of these techniques your presentations will have the kind of impact you want (Presumed Thought)."

Presuppositions of Language is where your language presupposes some previous knowledge or experience. Example, "You *are about to learn* something new.", suggests that the speaker is going to be sharing something that you are not experienced in. Or, "Are you *still trying the old methods* that have not resulted in success?", presupposes that the listener has been doing things from some period of time that are not working.

A **Universal Quantifier** is a word or set of words with a very generalized meaning and generally accepted or understood by all. For example, "*All the things that we can do* to effect a positive result are included in my proposal." If the listener accepts the language, then they must also accept that all the tasks and options are covered.

Modal Operators are our rules for life and presuppose *necessity* or *possibility*. "It is *imperative* that we think through our options before making a decision", states that the speaker believes this is an absolute must-do. If the listener accepts the statement, then they too will make the same assumption.

Simple Deletion is where some portion of the sentence is missing, leaving the listener to fill in the missing word for themselves. One might say, "You might be arriving at the idea that we need to take this proposal to the next step *and you can* when you see how our solution gives you the results you are looking for." What exactly is 'and you can' referring to here? 'Can' what? Arrive at the idea? Take the next step? It is difficult to tell.

A **Tag Question** is the salesman's go to question. "You can see this working for you, *right*?" "This is a very close match for you, *isn't it*? You could make this decision, *can you not*?

The **Yes Set** is where you pace the listener's external experience in such a way that they cannot deny the accuracy of what you are saying and then you insert new information. The human mind is much like a flywheel. Once it gets going in a particular direction, it tends to want to stay on the same course. Have you ever had a song stuck in your head? To execute a Yes Set you might say something like, "You have decided to improve your communication skills (yes) and so you have been working your way through this book (yes), and having read this far (yes), you have already learned some new techniques (implied yes)."

The **Double Bind** is the parent's best friend. "Would you like to clean your room now or in fifteen minutes?" It gives the listener the freedom to choose either of two options, both of which are preferable to you. "Will that be cash or charge?" The outcome remains as you would want it.

An **Implicit Request** takes the form of a question which requires only a 'yes' or 'no' answer, however, it often has the listener doing what it you would like them to do. For example, "Can you close the door?", should only require a 'yes' or 'no' yet, typically the listener will go close the door. It gives the listener the option to choose to respond and avoids authoritarianism on your part.

You can borrow someone else's authority by use of **Extended Quotation**. The technique simply calls out the quote from a well-known authority on a topic and never explains when their particular quote ended. For example, "A number of years ago, I was speaking with a friend and mentor in public speaking and he was telling me that Zig Ziglar said, 'To reach the heart and mind of a person, you must tell them a story.' *Stories are the mechanism which we inspire people to great things and when you tell stories...*" The previous sentence in *italics* represents what the speaker injected without telling the listener that Ziglar was no longer being quoted.

I recommend you take each one of these Indirect Language patterns and practice them for a day then move on to the next. When you have them down and fully understand how each works, begin to use them consciously and purposefully. The result will be that you will purposefully induce the listener to create information in their own mind and that is much more meaningful than you telling them the information directly.

Others: Chapter 2

Understanding Others

"If you talk to a man in a language he understands, that goes to his head. If you talk to him in his language, that goes to his heart."

Nelson Mandela

Who are you talking to?

Have you ever had someone talk *at you* rather than *to you*? You can hear this person talking... and you understand all the words... but the words don't all seem to fit together. It's as if they bounce off your ear back into the room, never making it inside your head.

This chapter could be a whole book in itself! People are fascinating in their variations and, the better you understand this, the better your communication can be with each person. Remember that it is important to stay externally focused on your audience. To do that, you need to understand whom you are talking to and structure your presentation so each person in the room can receive it.

Every person in your audience is different in every way from every other person in the room. The good news is that we can all be lumped into four general categories or speaking styles based on how we process information.

Language Styles

Words are tools. We each use the kind of tools that we are most familiar with in order to get the result we are looking for. When we don't use the right tool, we may still accomplish our task but it will take more effort. If you have ever tried to drive a small nail with the heel of a shoe or the back of a screwdriver, you know what I am talking about.

Suppose you and I were building a house together. You might be an expert with using a hammer while I might be the pro when it comes to the cordless screwdriver. If we are building a house together, it helps me to know that you prefer a hammer, or I will go to the store and buy a bunch of screws for the job. When I present these screws to you, it may take you a moment to decide how you are going to use all these screws when you brought your best hammer to the job. All the while I am thinking, 'Why the heck would anyone use a hammer when a screw is so much easier with a cordless screw driver?'

Perhaps you have noticed that certain people will tend to favor a certain language style in their speaking. One person may talk about how things *look* and how they *see* things, while another may talk about how they *feel* about something or how something feels in their hands.

Certainly, everyone knows what I mean when I say, "I *see* what you mean" however, a person who prefers to use a *visual* language style will truly understand it without having to unconsciously translate it. A person using a feeling language style will still 'get it' once they make the translation inside their own head. This takes some level of effort on the part of the listener. You, being the excellent presenter that you are, can take the burden off the listener by speaking their language.

Because the audience will contain people who speak and listen in all the different styles, an excellent presenter will utilize each of the styles during his presentation. These styles are; Visual, Auditory, Feeling, and Non-specific.

Visual

The first of the styles is visual. Visual people understand their world in a way that is associated with pictures. A visual person will describe their thoughts and experiences in terms of what they saw.

"I *saw* what you did there. You *brilliantly showed* me how to *clearly* make the best of my situation. I *look forward to seeing* this through."

Auditory

An auditory person will process their world through the association of sound. They will describe their thoughts and experiences in terms of hearing and sound qualities.

"I *hear* you. You *told* me how to *harmonize* what I am doing with my situation. It *sounds like* the best thing for me to do."

Feeling

A feeling person will process their world through the association of emotion, touch, or doing. They will describe their thoughts and experiences in terms of how they feel emotionally, what they feel through the sense of touch (tactile), and what they are doing.

"I'm *picking this up*. You *laid down* some great ideas. I *feel good about using this to make* the best of my situation. I am ready to *take action* now and *get it* done."

Non-Specific

A non-specific person will process their world by intellectualizing. They will describe their thoughts and experiences in terms of what makes sense and what is right or wrong. The language may seem like something you would hear from an old stodgy college professor, revealing little experiential content.

"I *understand* this. Your *processes let me realize what is right* in this situation. I *think* this is best."

Utilizing Speaking Styles

In one-on-one communication, it is important to first listen to what you hear the other person say then evaluate it as one of the four speaking styles; visual, auditory, feeling, or non-specific. Usually you will hear various words that represent two or more speaking styles. This is typical, as most people will say something like; "*I'm getting it now. You cleverly created a way for me harmonize the situation. I'm looking forward to seeing this through.*" You must reach beyond the words and see if you notice a particular style they tend to use most often, then utilize it in your speech.

When speaking to two or three people, you can determine their specific styles and utilize those in your discussion.

When speaking to groups, you will find that all four styles are represented so, being the excellent presenter that you are, you will be sure to use all four speaking styles in your presentation.

Learning Styles

There is an *Experiential Learning Theory* postulated by David and Alice Kolb that utilizes styles of how people learn. These learning styles are; Meaning, Concepts, Skills, and Adaptations.

The Meaning leaning style utilizes relevance within the experience to help form understanding. This learning style is curious about WHY something is important.

The Concepts learning style utilizes content within the experience to help form understanding. This learning style is seeking WHAT something is or is not.

The Skills learning style utilizes processes within the experience to help form understanding. This learning style is wondering HOW something works or is done.

The Adaptations learning style utilizes refinement of the experience to help form understanding. This learning style is exploring WHAT IF the circumstances change.

David and Alice Kolb strongly state that putting a person into one of these buckets should be avoided. Each person utilizes all these styles and, they will tend to favor one more than another. For our purposes, we will talk about people being WHY, WHAT, HOW, and WHATIF types as a way of describing their preference.

The key to creating a successful presentation, speech, sale... or any form of communication... is to present your information in the order the listener requires it. Doing so satisfies the listener's process for learning by first offering motivation for why they should listen. Now that you have their attention and they are listening, the second chunk of information explains definitions, jargon, and general content. At this point, the listener understands what you are talking about and their curiosity should be aroused. The third chunk of information is about the process of how to do what you are describing. Lastly, the fourth chunk of information is to offer some time for the listener to reflect on what they have heard or for you to present alternatives.

The 4-MAT system, developed by Bernice McCarthy, extends Kolb into a way of effective teaching. A wonderful byproduct is that it is also an effective way of presenting! You will learn more about 4-MAT in **Content: Chapter 4**.

Meta-Programs

One of the secrets to creating charisma is to be able to speak the language of the listener. Another secret is to be able to present the information in a way that is relevant and meaningful to them. When you have a group of people you are presenting too, you must be very flexible in meeting each person in their methods for how they process information.

The more you understand about your audience and build the presentation content while putting yourself in their shoes, the better your presentation will go.

Each member of the audience is running a set of 'meta-programs' for how they process information. These meta-programs are the underlying rules for how we select and process information. As an example, think about how you know you have done something very well. Perhaps you know that you did because someone told you (external) or perhaps you know because you just know inside yourself (internal). Some people *believe* they have done a good job, but it isn't until someone else tells them so that they actually *know* they did a good job (internal with an external check).

The first of the meta-programs are described in the Myers-Brigs Type Indicator;

- **I**ntroverts – **E**xtroverts
- i**N**tuitives – **S**ensors
- **T**hinkers – **F**eelers
- **J**udgers – **P**erceivers

There has been so much good content written on these meta-programs so I will leave it to you for additional reading on these however, I think it is important to talk about Judgers and Perceivers as it relates to motivating people into action.

Judgers like to make, and work from, lists. An electronic calendar is the perfect tool for the Judger who prefers to always know what they are doing and when they are doing it. Knowing there is a process and order to how things must be done will motivate the Judger into action.

Perceivers are the opposite of their Judger counterparts. The Perceiver uses lists and electronic calendars because they simply could not function effectively without it. The Perceiver likes to enjoy what is happening in the moment. To motivate a Perceiver, they need to know that *right now* is the last opportunity to make a decision and, by making the decision, they will have more options available to them. Perceivers love their options!

Judgers like structure. Perceivers do not.

Knowing whom you are talking to, the Judger or the Perceiver, means that you can apply the correct technique to help move them to action. In a group, you will have Judgers and Perceivers so you will need to speak to both of these needs for taking action.

Other meta-programs help you structure your language in such a way as to make it more meaningful and more motivational.

The Direction meta-program describes if the listener tends to be more motivated *towards* something or perhaps, they are motivated *away from* something. This is a simple application of the carrot or the stick in order to get action. Any effective presentation should cover the benefits of taking action on what you are presenting as well as spell out the consequences.

The Reason meta-program describes if a person does what they do out of *possibility* or out of *necessity*. Your presentation should appeal to both.

The Convincer Demonstration meta-program describes how often or how many times a person needs to see, hear, or otherwise experience success with what you are describing in order for them to be convinced. By far, the most common is the 3-time convincer. Most people need to hear your offer or benefit 3 times before they are convinced.

The Chunk Size meta-program describes how specific or abstract a person needs information in order to process content. Most of the population needs to see the big picture first before they receive the details. By getting the big picture, they better understand the content and relationships of the specific bits of information.

The Listening Style meta-program describes if a person is more likely to take what you say literally or if they interpret your presentation metaphorically. There seems to be a correlation in business to take things quite literally and this becomes even more critical as the parties are getting closer to contract discussions. Your presentation, given early in the relationship with the audience can be more inferential and it should contain some very literal points as well.

Why are they coming to your presentation?

Remember, 35% of your audience is likely to be most focused on WHY they are listening to you. What was it that compelled them to come listen to you? Are you a well-known speaker with a topic they are curious about? Perhaps their boss told them they had to be in your presentation. Maybe they need to buy your product and they think you're just-another-sales-guy gushing lines of prating sales dialog and marketing spin messages until the mind is numb.

You need to know why each person is in the room. What is their reason for being there? If you don't know, find out early. The more you know about each individual, the more you can customize your message or relate specific content to an individual. This enhances your rapport with each person and builds an affirmative response potential for your message.

Clearly, when there are more people in the room than you can meet, make it a point to meet as many as you can. Focus on those that appear to be the leaders or key people in the room. This is a good time to ask for introductions by the person who brought you in for the presentation.

One way I meet people before giving a presentation is by hanging out with the audience beforehand. This is a great time to begin establishing rapport while at the same time, you are learning about their specific interests.

Engage people in conversation and see if you can discover what it is that they want to learn from your presentation so you can map your talking points to that. Make it a point to know why they are there and utilize that during your presentation.

If you are doing a sales presentation, learn the prospect's reasons for being there. Your reason, or your boss' reason, is not important. You must understand why the prospect is there and what they want to gain from the encounter.

With all the knowledge you can pull from this informal setting, you can tailor your message to include things you learned and attribute that portion of your message to the person from which you learned it.

"I was talking with Megan (while giving a look or open hand gesture toward Megan) *before the presentation and she told me to make sure I communicated the value of being an excellent communicator. She said it would be one of my keys to success today. So let's make sure that is covered in detail. When you are an excellent communicator you can..."*

Megan and the rest of the audience now know you listened to the counsel you were given. They see that you followed up on it. They felt heard and cared for. This is a huge contributor to building rapport and giving credibility to your presentation.

Communicating: Chapter 3

How Communication Works

"The single biggest trouble in communication is the illusion that it has taken place."

George Bernard Shaw

It's all in your head...

People are meaning-making creatures. Given any amount of data, the human mind will attempt to fill in the gaps and construct some form of meaning. Any unfulfilled meaning leaves the unconscious mind in a state of excitation and if it cannot fill the gap, it begins constructing multiple options based on personal experience in an attempt to make sense out of the data. Even when all the data is present, the end result of the communication is still likely to be muddled because it is always processed through the filter of the listener's personal experience.

If this is enough explanation for you then move ahead to the next chapter. If you like to know the bits and bytes of how and why this is the case, continue reading.

In the excellent book *Flow,* on the psychology of optimal experience, Mihaly Csikszentmihalyi says that we process about two million bits of information at any one point in time. Those two million bits are processed through the filters of *delete, distort,* and *generalize* so that we now have a reasonable volume of data to experience as our reality. In fact, it is estimated that two million bits of information could be deleted, distorted, and generalized down to just 126 bits of information.

I think it is easy to agree that on this basis alone, it is quite likely that, while we may think we have communicated effectively, we have in fact been misunderstood to some degree.

All decision-making and meaning-making is done in the conscious and unconscious minds. The conscious mind is responsible for logical thought while the unconscious is the domain of memories and emotions. The joining of these two functions is ultimately how we create what we *think* we understand. Confusing? Nah... let's break it down

The Conscious Mind and Decision-Making

The conscious mind is actually quite easy to understand. If a decision needs to be made, it is the job of the conscious mind. The conscious mind also processes the Boolean logic of *not*, *or*, and *and.*

The conscious mind is concerned with *rationalization*. It takes the meaning formed in the unconscious mind and layers in additional data and rules for processing that data. Sometimes the end result is desired and other times it is not. Perhaps you have experienced something like this... You're driving down the road looking for that great restaurant you found a month or so ago. You arrive at a tee in the road where you must turn right or left. This isn't familiar but you just somehow know you should turn left. As you look to the right, it seems like you remember going that way. "After all, it should be closer to the lake", you justify to yourself. The decision is made, and you take the right turn. Three miles later you say, "This isn't the right way". You make a U-turn and find your destination just half a mile past where you made the inaccurate decision to turn right. As you pull into the parking lot you exclaim, "I just *knew* I should have turned left!"

Yeah, I know... I've done it too.

Albert Einstein said, "The intuitive mind is a sacred gift and the rational mind is a faithful servant. We have created a society that honors the servant and has forgotten the gift." How much more could we do if we gave full trust and confidence to the unconscious mind while giving congruent and meaningful direction from the conscious mind?

The Unconscious Mind and Meaning-Making

The unconscious mind is a deep well of mystery that has been a continuous study since man became sentient. Within the unconscious we find streams of emotions, memories, thoughts, and dreams all merging into rivers of data on demand with no concern or need of rationalization.

Remember, the unconscious mind is where *meaning* is formed. As an excellent communicator, you must understand the basic rules for how the unconscious mind processes information. With this knowledge, you can construct your language in such a way as to create the best opportunity for the listener to truly understand.

One of the components of meaning-making is deciphering the speaker's feeling and attitude about what he says. Albert Mehrabian, as of this writing is a Professor Emeritus of Psychology at UCLA. He has become known best by his publications on the importance of verbal and nonverbal messages. Mehrabian says that 55% of our feeling and attitude is communicated in our facial expression. Our tone of voice makes up 38% of this communication of feeling and attitudes, and words are only 7%.

If you do your research on Mehrabian you will find that there is an often-misapplied application of his 7-38-55 rule in explaining how the transmission of *meaning* is created in a communication. Well, I am going to do the same misapplication of his rule only for the benefit of making sense of how much more significant tonality is than words; and body language is more significant than both words and tonality combined. Remember, Mehrabian was talking about how we express our congruence of feelings and attitudes. We are applying the same idea to how we communicate *meaning*. I hope Mr. Mehrabian will forgive me.

If words are only 7% then it stands to reason that we should become conscious of how we are communicating the 93% of meaning so as to ensure we are better understood. In **Chapter 6, Delivering Your Presentation**, I'll cover the art of how to effectively use Body Language.

If your presentation is face-to-face either in person or via video then you have the full benefit of body language, tonality, and words in order to establish meaning.

If your presentation is online without video your ability to establish meaning is reduced to tonality and words, however, body language, on your part is still very important. As an excellent communicator, you still maintain your physiology just as you do in a face-to-face conversation. Sitting or standing in a posture that communicates astute knowledge and resourcefulness will come across in your tonality.

By far, the most limiting form of communication is simple text like email – or even this book. Words make up only 7% of the communication of the speaker's feelings and attitudes. That means that even reading this book you do not have the benefit of seeing me talk about this topic nor can you listen to my tone of voice to help better understand me. You are using only 7% in order to make meaning of what I say.

How then do you effectively create meaning and understanding out of what you read? Here is the tricky part... your unconscious mind likes complete packages of information. In fact, when information is left out or otherwise missing, your unconscious mind will make it up! That's right. Any missing information is made up and the blanks are filled in.

Are you aware that you have holes in your field of vision called blind-spots? Where the optic nerve attaches to your retina there are no rods or cones to pick up light in that region. You are literally quite blind and there are two black holes, one for each eye, in your field of vision. Why do you not see them then? Because your brain makes up for the missing information and colors it in so-to-speak. If you want to find your blind-spot, you find a YouTube video to show you how. It is easy to do.

In order to develop your meaning of what I have written on this page, you have to fill in the 93% of missing information that would otherwise come from my tonality and my body language. Where do you get this otherwise missing information? *You get it from your own mind.* That's right! Even as you are reading this book, you impress upon these words and, to some extent upon me, whatever feelings or attitudes you have right now and that determines your understanding of what I have written.

This then explains why we developed punctuation and certain grammatical structures to help the meaning-making in written communication. Certainly "Help.", "Help!", and "HELP!" all convey a need for assistance yet, it is easy to understand that they do so with differing levels of urgency.

Even in today's electronic-age many people use emoticons to help convey feelings and attitudes. Or do they? ;-)

Say What?

What you say is not as important as how you say it. Only 7% as it turns out! And... it is even less than that really. Words have no meaning except the meaning we choose to give them and even that changes over time.

In the United States in the 1940's, everyone wanted to be 'gay'. Not so true anymore. In the 40's, to be gay was to be happy. Today, I have a hard time keeping up with what is 'hot' or what is 'cool'. Is 'sick' or 'phat' good or do I need to call a doctor? Certainly, if something is 'gnarly', I should at least call a carpenter and get it fixed.

The words themselves do not establish meaning. It is *your perception* of the meaning of those words that create the meaning and that meaning is derived from the tonality, body language, and more importantly, the context in which the word is used.

There is so much that goes into the creation of meaning that a whole academic textbook could be written on the subject. If you want to understand this in great detail, I would encourage you to make a formal study into *Neuro-linguistic Programming* (NLP). Specifically, I would refer you to Magic of NLP Demystified by Pucelik and Lewis.

For our purposes as excellent presenters, we can stay focused on two key elements of how a listener makes-meaning of your presentation and therefore, arrives at his or her understanding of what you are saying.

1. All communication results in a series of pictures in the listener's mind.
2. These pictures carry a vast amount of ever-changing information, **which is the meaning of your presentation, as they know it.**

All of this loose structure of meaning-making for a person to arrive at *understanding* leads us to one simple truth; your skills as a masterful communicator are defined by the extent of your control over the pictures in the mind of your listener.

It is not so simple to tell a person to make certain pictures in their mind. You have to induce the listener to create the picture you want them to have in their mind. Your process for doing this is to give the picture life in the form of a story.

Dr. Anne Foerst, the author of *God in the Machine*, is a theologian and researcher at the Artificial Intelligence Laboratory at MIT. She says that our classification as Homo Sapiens is not necessarily unique and therefore not the best categorization for human beings.

What does make the human animal unique among all other animals is that humans tell stories. We know other animals communicate. It appears however, that they only communicate information. Humans communicate *experience* and they do it in the form of a story.

Since the dawn of the human mind, storytelling has captivated attention, formed opinions, cultivated meaning, and developed understanding. Stories have moved nations to war, and they have moved societies to compassion. The *story* allows the human to develop the experience within his own mind. Once developed, the experience is, to some degree, made real in the mind. It is through the processing of this experience that the human moves beyond just understanding something, into the capability of realization – that act of applying the understanding in new ways to spontaneously create new knowledge.

As humans, we go through a process of learning that begins with not even knowing what we don't know and ends with mastery.

There are four steps to learning;

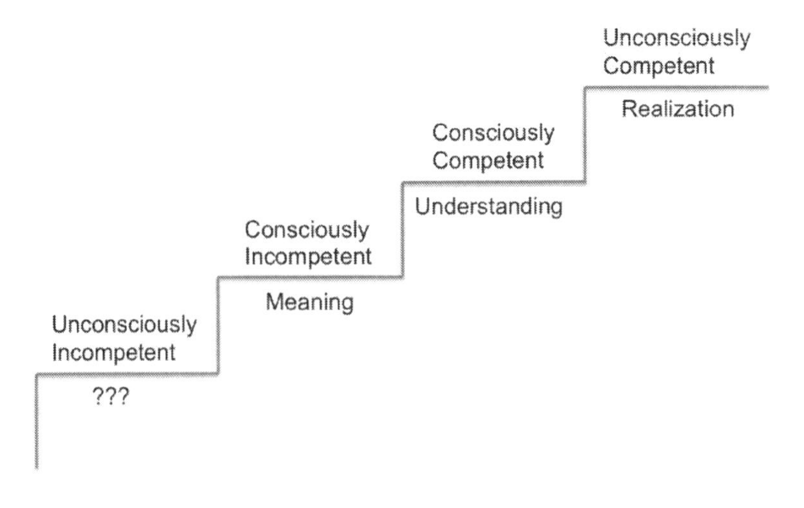

Step One: Unconsciously Incompetent – You don't know what you don’t know. The fact that there is something to learn here is not even in your awareness. At some point in your life, probably when you were quite young, you had no idea that a car existed or even what a car was for. You were unconsciously incompetent with respect to driving.

Step Two: Consciously Incompetent – At this step, you have become aware and are now creating meaning out of your new knowledge. My grandson, Brayden, is three years old at the time of this writing. He knows that when he and his mom go to Grandmommie’s house, they get in the car. He will sit in his car seat in the middle of the back seat and when mom turns the big circle in front of her, the car moves in that direction and from time to time, he imitates that. He also knows that when the light turns green, he is supposed to say, “Come on people. Let's move it!” If you tell him to get in the front seat and drive, he will look at you incredulously and say, “You know I can’t drive.”

Step Three: Consciously Competent – Now true learning is occurring, and you are developing understanding. In this step, much focus and attention are given to the learning process. Remember when you were learning to drive a car? Sitting in the driver's seat for the time, it felt a little odd and unfamiliar. It even felt a little scary because you knew that you had not yet mastered the process. Your hands griped tightly at 'ten and two'. One foot pressed the clutch and another the brake. Your eyes focused straight ahead while your brain ran through the infinite ways you were to release the brake and apply pressure to the accelerator while gently letting out the clutch. You didn't want anyone to talk to you... that would just be way too much for you to process at one time.

Step Four: Unconsciously Competent – In this step, you have completed the learning process. What that means, is that the learnings are so much a part of your unconscious mind that you don't even need to think about what it is that you are doing. You just do it. As an adult now, you get in your car, start it up, and drive off without giving any consideration or concern about *how to drive* your car.

Now you have true learning and have moved beyond just understanding how a car is driven. You actually realize, in real time, *how* to drive the car. So long as your car is performing normally, there is nothing to do but drive. What happens when you notice a strange noise or if the steering does not work correctly? You actually go back momentarily into Step Three, Consciously Competent, until you understand the new characteristics of how your car is performing. Once you have assimilated this new knowledge, you move into Step Four again. Likewise, when you rent a car, or borrow a friend's car, you can quickly assimilate the information about this car and *realize* how to drive it.

How do you know when you have achieved Unconscious Competence? When you explain it someone else and you have to pause to think about it, then explain in great detail how the act is done, you have achieved Unconscious Competence. Try explaining to someone on the other end of the telephone how to tie his shoes!

Realization is the act of dynamically and unconsciously applying existing knowledge in new ways in order to create solutions or new knowledge. You were taught that 2 + 2 equals 4 and at some point, you so completely understood the concept of addition that you could realize the answer to any two numbers added together.

In your presentation – in any communication – your objective is to get the listener to realize, in his own mind, what it is that you are saying. You want him to create the picture in his own mind the way you want, and you want him to be able to do that in such a way as to make it meaningful to himself or his situation. That is the essence of communication.

When the words you speak, embellished with a congruent tonality and body language, weave a captivating story that establish a series of pictures or thoughts in the mind of the listener and that results in him producing the response you desire... THAT is effective communication! That is how communication works.

Content: Chapter 4

Preparing Your Presentation Content

"Before anything else, preparation is the key to success."

Alexander Graham Bell

Build a Strong Foundation

If you are going to build something that will last in the mind of your audience, it is necessary to build a strong foundation upon which you will lay the brick and mortar of your words and actions. A little planning goes a long way and will ensure that your presentation is well formed to accomplish your goals.

The great edifices built by man still stand because they were created with purpose and are built upon solid foundations; so too with the great speeches of man. Rarely does an extemporaneously performed speech or presentation make it into the history books. In laying the foundation for your presentation, consider where you can add humor, storytelling, curiosity, anticipation, facts, and brainstorming. All of these entice the engagement of the human mind and they lead to the entrancing of your audience.

On November 19th, 1863, Abraham Lincoln offered a memorable two-minute speech at Soldiers' National Cemetery in Gettysburg, Pennsylvania. Even this short speech was carefully prepared albeit on scrap paper. It made such an impact on the national consciousness that on August 28th, one hundred years later, Dr. Martin Luther King delivered another nation-shaping oration. The *'I have a Dream'* speech was not only delivered from the steps of the Lincoln Memorial, but Lincoln, Jefferson, and other well-known orators heavily influenced it. Dr. King built the foundation of his speech by utilizing the well-established foundation of others.

Prepare Your Content

As you begin to prepare the content of your presentation, the first thing to consider is why *you* are there. What is the outcome you desire for this presentation? Make sure that you are creating the content designed to get the outcome you intend. Remember, if you do not know where you are going then any road you take will be just fine. In order to benefit from your effort, you must have a well-defined outcome.

The next item to consider in preparing your content is the audience you are addressing and why they have come to listen to you. It is imperative to understand why they are there so you can satisfy, or at least contribute to, their desire.

The totality of a successful presentation is dependent on knowing the listener's purpose for attending and your purpose for speaking. These are the most important steps in preparing for a successful presentation.

Next, make a list of what you want to say. You may choose to do this by means of an outline or perhaps you will jot some notes. List out the important elements you want to cover. Let's make this an exercise. Get out some paper and a pen or pencil (or open a new document) and write a list of what you want to cover in your presentation. Once you have the list, sequence the items into a logical order. In a few minutes, you will re-sequence them using a formal structure. For now, just get the ideas lined up in the order you want to cover them.

Equally important to what you want to say is what you ***DO NOT*** want to say. Thinking of what you know about the audience, make a 'NO List' of sensitive topics or facts that might upset them. Check with coworkers and others who might have knowledge about the attendees and add those items to the list. Now, go through your list of items you want to cover and make sure there are no conflicts with items in the 'NO List'. If you find a conflict and the topic must be covered, have a mitigation plan to defuse any potential negative situation and get the presentation back on track.

Now that you have your two lists, look at the content strategically. Does it meet your purpose and the purpose of the attendees? If so, you are now ready to build your content for presentation.

4-MAT

The 4-MAT system of organizing information created by McCarthy and Kolb is an exquisite way of assembling your content into structured chunks of information that serves each person in the room in the order they prefer to be served. You can use 4-MAT as a way to make sure that each person in the room gets the information they need, in the order they need it, so they can develop a full understanding of your content. This is effective anytime you are offering the listener a sale or a change of mind.

When you use 4-MAT, more people will walk up to you after your presentation with good questions and comments and; you will reduce the number of questions that interrupt your presentation.

It is one thing to hear someone speak while it is entirely different to listen. Hearing is simply the act of processing and recognizing sound without assigning meaning to the sound. Listening, on the other hand, processes what is heard into some cognitive understanding.

Have you ever sat in a presentation and after 15 minutes began to ask yourself, "Why am I here?" and "What the heck is this all about?" Perhaps you even rationalized that the speaker is using a lot of important buzzwords, but you still don't get the point of the presentation. 4-MAT is the tool you need to structure your presentation into blocks, or chunks, of information that your attendees are looking for.

4-MAT is organizing your information into four blocks of content; WHY, WHAT, HOW, and WHATIF.

You can make a handy outline to help you organize your content into 4MAT by taking a sheet of paper and dividing it into four sections. Label each section appropriately as WHY, WHAT, HOW, WHATIF. In each section, make notes or bullet lists appertaining to the content you will discuss in that section.

WHY

Roughly 35% of your audience will be WHY (or even WHY NOT) people and they like discussions. Their primary learning mode is through brainstorming and interacting. They need to understand the motivation behind what you are presenting. These people will not even begin to listen until they know WHY they must listen. WHY people are reflective observers and they operate best when they are led into action by the presenter. They need reasons and relevance for what they are doing.

WHY people need to know upfront *why they should listen to you* and *why your content is useful* before they will even begin the process of listening. This person needs a mental container to hold what you are about to give them.

Imagine your audience has come into the room and there they sit waiting to be served a nice cup of tea... and no one brought a cup with them. You need to provide the cup. This is the WHY of your presentation. It gives them a reason to listen and therefore a real opportunity to learn from what you are saying.

On your 4-MAT outline, make a list of why the listener wants this information... why it is important... why it is beneficial. Remember, *relevance* is the key.

WHAT

About 22% of your audience will be WHAT people. They are also reflective observers and they require little to no interaction. 'Just the facts' is their motto.

A WHAT person gets their knowledge by analyzing, classifying, and theorizing and they need information to do that. Their learning process is more internal.

Your next chunk of information on your 4-MAT outline is to define the WHAT of what you are presenting. Be sure you define any jargon you will be using while you layout the descriptive narrative of your content. Provide examples through stories and offer counterexamples.

Your goal in the WHAT section is to give *information.* Some people just want the details. They do not want, or need, you to tell them how to do it. They would rather throw out the instruction book and figure it out themselves or have someone else do it. Keep in mind that all of your attendees will need to have the underlying details of what you are discussing. This lets them apply the information in a way that is relevant to their needs.

On your 4-MAT outline, make a bullet list of information you want to communicate to your audience and any jargon that needs to be defined or explained.

HOW

The smallest group in your audience is the doers. They are the HOW people and they make up 18% of those in attendance. HOW people are active in the learning process. They need to know how something is done and the specific steps involved. HOW people will tinker and experiment with things and they have a keen interest in improving them too.

HOW people are more patient, and they will sit quietly until you get into their section. They find the WHY and the WHAT content interesting but, they really need to know the process. Their patience can run out though. If they feel you have belabored the information enough, they may try and take control of your presentation by asking questions about how they can use your information.

The third chunk of information in the sequence of your presentation is HOW to use what you have presented in the WHAT content.

The HOW section is a step-by-step description of what to do. An enumerated list of steps is especially appreciated by the HOW people.

On your 4-MAT outline, write out the steps you want the audience to do and the order you want them to do them.

WHATIF

The last group in your audience at 25% are the WHATIF people. These folks are also active in the learning process and they like to modify and adapt what you are saying into other situations and scenarios.

The WHATIF people are the most patient of the whole group and may not say a word until it is Q&A time. When that time comes, the WHATIF people will fire off their questions often derived from some random or unusual situation they have dreamed up in their mind. It is through the questioning process, and the teaching of others, that the WHATIF people learn.

This Q&A process lets them assemble the information in alternative ways for themselves. The simplest way to satisfy this part of the 4-MAT outline is to ask for questions. Often, people can be hesitant to be the first to speak up. If you have two or three questions ready to go, that will prime the pump and get your audience thinking and talking.

Slide Presentations (PowerPoint and Keynote)

While this is certainly not a 'how to' book for PowerPoint or any other slide or presentation tool, it is worth a mention on how to effectively utilize slides.

Slides should be used for one purpose in your presentation, to clarify and enhance what you are saying. The most prevalent mistake made with slides is to put all of the content on the slides and allow the slide to drive the presentation. There is probably no faster way to have your audience check out of your presentation. If you are reading your slides, they can just read them too. You are not needed.

A 'pro' presenter will use slides to draw the audience's attention to the points of discussion being made. You should have a sparse amount of information and minimize use of flashy animations that can be distracting. The key to animations is to make sure they support the content and add meaning. Imagine a slide with a bullet list of how to create successful presentations and every letter appears with some nifty animations. The sparkling, growing, turning, color-changing text used will likely cause your audience to lose connection with you, the presenter, and the meaning behind the content of your presentation.

A 'super-ninja' presenter will make effective use of graphics and animations in order to visually stimulate the audience and illustrate the content of your message. Imagine that rather than a bullet list of how to create successful presentations; you have a diagram or flowchart that visually walks the audience through the process.

By combining animations and running them simultaneously, it is possible to create some impressive visual effects that are not otherwise possible in one animation. I have a very complex slide I use in many of my trainings that visually demonstrates to the audience how our brain processes events and stores them with a concept of time. I show this slide while I am talking about the process. There are no words on the slide, just images. Initially, the slide presents the idea that time is stored in a linear manner as a 'timeline'. Then, objects appear on the screen and move to specific locations in the timeline causing a visual change indicating that the process has completed. Some of those objects are larger when they first appear on the screen then shrink when they move into the timeline as if they are moving farther away. This slide took me 8 hours to build. The payoff in student comprehension has been well worth the time spent and I look like a pro with well-prepared content.

The final word on slides is, use them if they help you get your point across. Slides are built for your audience and help your audience discover the meaning of your presentation at a deeper level. If you are using slides as a crutch, get rid of them and learn your content.

Setup: Chapter 5

Get Set to Deliver Your Presentation

"All things are ready, if our mind be so."

William Shakespeare

Setup the Space

As you get ready for the delivery of your presentation consider the setup of the room. This may be in your control and if it is, strategically consider where you want the screen, projector, tables, flipcharts, and even the audience. Perhaps you want key decision-makers to sit in certain places. If you have the ability to change the room, lighting, temperature, or anything else that stacks the deck in your favor, do it.

If the room setup is not in your control, make the best of what you have and change what you can. Treat this space as another of your tools to deliver an amazing presentation.

If the presentation is a long seminar or training that will last more than 4 hours, I prefer to visit the location the evening before and setup if possible. For multi-day presentations or trainings, this is a good option. Just a simple presentation may mean that you can only get in a little early and setup. Often, we are in a situation where there is no access before presentation time. In this case, do the best you can with what you have.

I recommend you bring your own equipment whenever possible and it is reasonable to do so. For example, I always carry a small LCD-type projector with me. It is surprising how often I meet with small groups in a conference room with no projector, or the projector is so old, the quality of my presentation suffers. Once I was escorted into such a conference room and half the image made by the projector had a sickly-green tint across the bottom-half of my presentation. Even though it was not my equipment, the unconscious perception by the attendees was that my presentation looked less than professional. Since then, I carry my own projector.

For bigger presentations, if you are using music, lighting, or other embellishments, make sure they are setup and ready to go. If you have assistants, be sure everyone is briefed on the start time as well as their duties. A checklist is a good idea for these larger presentations.

Prepare Your Mind

Before you go in to start your presentation prepare your mind. Put on your headphones or if you are using a sound system, play your theme song. Turn it up! You are why they have come. You are *The Rockstar... The Perfect Host... The Double Agent.* The party is wherever *you* are. Have a little swagger in your step. Be confident in yourself, your material, and your product. People love you because you help them get what they want.

Get your head right. You will know you're ready when your body tells you so. You should be calm and confident in a relaxed body.

As you enter the room to greet those in attendance, or to begin your presentation, be present in the moment. Allow your gaze to soften by activating your peripheral vision and remain in this state even as you are making eye contact with others (see **Relax!** in Chapter One). Stay outwardly focused so each person you meet feels you are there for him or her personally.

Establishing Rapport

Rapport is another key to successful communication between two individuals. It is the condition where a bond of trust is formed, and the words spoken are more readily accepted by the listener with little critical analysis. This is not to mean the listener agrees. They may not but they did accept what you had to say.

When you have the opportunity to mingle with the audience prior to your presentation, you can work to establish rapport by allowing your body, speech, and mannerisms to become like the person you are speaking with. During the handshake, give back what you get from them in pressure and style of handshake. If they are smiling, put a smile on your face. If they are sitting, adopt a similar sitting posture. Stand in a similar stance as they have. All of these things lead to building a feeling of comfort and familiarity between people and establish rapport.

Your Introduction

If you are on a panel or participating in a business presentation where multiple people are introducing themselves, you can leverage this as an opportunity to set the tone for the meeting in your favor.

If you're first to introduce yourself, keep it brief. If you're not first, follow the format the others are using but take less time than anyone else - set a new tone. Let the audience know you are there to serve them. In their mind, this is about them, not you. Establish your authority on the subject at hand or on the outcome of the meeting. Establishing relevance for your content and why you are the expert on the matter.

Oh yeah... If this is a business presentation, take those marketing slides about how long your company has been in business and how much revenue you made over the last 5 years and move them to the back of the slides.

Opening Stories

When appropriate, opening with a story or metaphor can be very powerful. Your story should be designed to capture the attention of your audience and draw them in to your words. By relating to the audience's situation and offering the hint of a solution, they will turn their focus to you and your presentation. Remember, every person there is interested in only how his or her personal experience will improve. If you are selling a product to an employee of a company, he or she is not interested in how your product is going to help the company; they want to know how it will help them.

Your story should also set the emotional resources your audience's needs for the rest of your presentation. If it would benefit your audience to be in states of; *curiosity*, *'it is possible'*, and *'I can do it'* then your opening story should contain these elements.

Metaphors can be a very powerful tool to set the atmosphere for your presentation and to preframe rules, expectations, or outcomes. Consider this brief opening story for a 'How to improve Your Sales' seminar;

"Thank you for the warm welcome. I am very excited about what we will accomplish together in the next two hours. You see, it wasn't that long ago I was in your shoes. I knew that I had to make changes in order to hit my sales targets, but I felt I didn't have the time or resources to do so. My manager started conducting weekly account reviews, providing more oversight and I was feeling the pressure to hit revenue targets. I was so ready to achieve my goals now that I was willing to take a chance. I had to find a new way of working and thinking in order to get better results. So, in 2005 I attended a presentation, much like this one. In that presentation I learned that it was possible, and even reasonable, to double my sales. I learned it was not about how hard or how much I worked or what sales process or closing technique I used. Instead, I learned it was more about how I communicated with people. It was about me helping people understand how they would achieve their goals and get the results ***they*** *were looking for. From that moment, I made a commitment to form new habits that were centered around making relationships and asking people to do what they desire. More than just asking them to do what they desired to do, I held them accountable for doing it. As a result of me committing two hours of my time and being willing and open to learning something new, I immediately saw improvement in my deal closure, my customers were more satisfied – some of them have even become great friends, and now, I feel I am working less while more than doubling my salary. I didn't do this for my family. I didn't do this*

for my boss or my employer. I did it for me. I did it because I want better, and I deserve better."

This story tells your audience that you identify with where they are and sends the message that they can improve their situation – and deserve to do so – just like you did. It has a positive message that suggests they too can double their sales and not have to work harder. This story inevitably leaves the listener with the question, "*How do you do that?*" If you can get them to ask that question aloud, or silently in their own mind, you have them. They are now listening.

Creating Expectation

At this point, you have made your introduction and set the tone for your presentation. You have created the condition for WHY people will listen to you. Now you need to build the expectations and 'rules of engagement' for your presentation. Do you want to take questions at a certain time? Is this to be interactive? What is the audience allowed to do? How will you engage with the audience?

It is a good idea to first build a desire within the audience for them to *want* to engage. Making a generalized statement that allows the listener to evaluate themselves as compared to others in their ability to be successful is a good way to light a fire under them.

Consider these:

"Not everybody is ready to do this."

"Only those in my class that know they are worthy of being successful get the best results."

"I find that my seminar participants who make decisions quickly are the ones that get the most out of this material."

I particularly like the first statement, "*Not everybody is ready to do this.*" It gives each person the opportunity to self-select out of the group thus eliminating wasted time, for themselves and for you, and it will minimize disruptions for other students. The implied situation for those remaining in the class is that they are ready and therefore, they are prepared to learn and take action. This necessitates that they listen and participate.

Setting the Frame for Your Presentation

Tell your audience what you are going to tell them. Let them know if this is a training session, seminar, presentation, discussion, or whatever other option you can think of. Let them know how far you plan to take the topic and what they can expect to gain from it.

By setting the frame, you are refining their expectation of the material and the end result they should expect. This enhances their satisfaction and helps to gain their buy-in.

Audience participation may be desired especially if your presentation is in a business setting or some type of training. If you desire the audience to engage, tell them so. From the beginning of your presentation ask them questions and request the audience to respond. Even asking for a hand response will get people to begin engaging.

A key to successful presentations is to make sure that expectations are set correctly. Missed expectations are the cause for disappointment.

The 'Magic Wand' Question

In a presentation where you are targeting your information to solve specific needs or requirements, like a sales presentation, you need to understand something of the nature of the problems they are dealing with. The challenge is getting your audience to give you the facts about the problem. Unless you have built a sufficient rapport and are seen as the Trusted Advisor, your attendees are not likely to 'air their dirty laundry' in public.

This brilliant little nugget comes from my friend, Don Aspromonte, in his excellent book, *Green Light Selling*. The 'Magic Wand' Question gives the audience the opportunity to put the surface level problems on the table, getting them out of the way, so they can tell you what the *real* problems are.

Consider the following dialog:

> *Presenter: Before I begin, I have one question that, while it may seem a little unusual, will help me best understand how I can help you. If you would please, consider this. If I were to give you a magic wand and you could wave that magic wand over your business (or other topic of discussion) to fix or improve anything, what would you fix or improve?*

Sales Mgr #1: Sales pipeline reporting. That is where we have the most problem. We don't know how our pipeline is aging and so we lose opportunities due to lack of follow-up.

Sales Mgr #2: I agree. I would also improve our sales process. We need to be more efficient, so we are responsive to prospect inquiries.

Sales Mgr #3: I think we need training. Our salespeople tend to skip regular training and as a result, do not stay up to date on product specs.

Presenter: Great information. Thank you. Mr. Sales VP, you have heard these thoughts. You now have the magic wand. What would you fix or improve?

VP Sales: I agree with my managers. All these things need to be done. I think they covered it.

Presenter: Excellent. Thank you. Now, assuming I can do all of that, is there anything else? At this point, shut up and wait. Eventually someone will speak up and probably add a new level of problem to the mix, something more important to them.

Sales Mgr #2: Well, if you can do ***that****, what I really think needs to be done is to enable our technical pre-sales staff with soft skills so our sales people can focus on closing deals rather than trying to get the customer to buy-in to the technology.*

You may get one or two deeper level concerns. Vet those with the attendees and address what you can in order to make a strong impression.

So… you got dragged into a presentation cold. Now what?

It happens. You're sitting at your desk and the boss calls. "*You're needed. Now! We have an important customer and didn't anticipate they want to talk about our upcoming release. Get down here as quick as you can*!"

As rare as this is (insert sarcastic tone and smiley face here) it happens and, the skilled presenter will handle this with ease and grace. All the steps mentioned above are important and to whatever extent possible, should be fulfilled. It is, however, sometimes difficult to do in this situation.

When you are brought in cold to do a presentation there are three things you must accomplish and in this order:

1. Establish Your Expertise

   Briefly explain to your audience your background and the reason you are the right person to be addressing them on this issue at this time.

2. Use the 'Magic Wand' Question

   "If I were to give you a magic wand and you could wave that magic wand over your business to fix or improve anything, what would you fix or improve?"

3. Use a conditional close question to quantify the objective to ensure success.

   "If I can do X for you now, would that be a good use of our time?"

At this point, everything in your presentation should be aligned to achieve the outcome they agreed with.

Execute: Chapter 6

Delivering Your Presentation

"I shall bere your noble fame, for ye spake a grete worde and fulfilled it worshipfully."

Sir Thomas Malory of Newbold Revel

Taking Care of Business

Finally, we arrive at the moment of execution. You have set the stage for your audience to listen. You have arranged your content, so it is easily consumed by the human mind. You have opened the presentation by introduction, set up the initial stories, created rapport, and have defined the frame for being successful in your presentation. The spotlight is on you... now is your moment to shine!

Now is the time to dive into your 4-MAT. The first thing you need to establish is the WHY. Remember, the WHY creates relevance for why the audience should listen.

Keep the energy level up as needed. In the role of presenter, you are part entertainer and part educator. It will be necessary for you to maintain the environment for optimal engagement of the attendees. You can do this through the use of humor, story-telling, body-language, direct and indirect language patterns, and the strategic use of tension.

One of the best ways to get the audience engaged is to interact with them. Get them to do something together as a group. For a smaller audience, you can ask questions and get back verbal responses. For larger audiences, you can ask for hand responses. For huge audiences, you can have them do things like stand up, take a deep breath, stretch, or say some positive responses, like "Yes!" or "Woo!" as a group. A prepared icebreaker might be useful as well.

I was attending a presentation once on using the power of desire to create focus. The presenter asked the audience to imagine something they had a strong desire to have. Then he had everyone stand and told them to put their hands in the air and shout, "I want it! I deserve it!" While people were looking at each other wondering if their neighbor was going to participate in this silly exercise, the presenter said, "There are two things you need to know before we begin. First, it's silly if only you do it by yourself. If we all do it then it's not silly [chuckles]. Second, if you are sitting down and not doing it then you are in the minority [chuckles]. Besides that, if you knew this would lead you to get what you most desired, would you stand up and shout, 'I want it! I deserve it!'?" I think everyone participated.

Humor is often useful to get an audience engaged, especially when talking to large audiences like a keynote address. If you can get a chuckle out of the audience every two minutes, they will stay engaged. Remember that humor is not always appropriate though. If the attendees are in a time crunch or perhaps the mood is not right, leave overt humor at the door. Audience size can also dictate your use of humor. It seems to me that for a smaller audience humor can detract from the message.

Sequencing and Chunking Information

As you pace through your content in 4-MAT you will want to be sure that it is sequenced logically, like a story. There should be a beginning, a middle, and a conclusion. In 4-MAT terms, your beginning is the WHY content, your middle is the WHAT content, and the conclusion is the HOW content.

People have an uncanny ability to store information sequentially. They like to know that *A* comes before *B* and *B* comes before *C*. If you suddenly go back and drop a new fact on them 'out of time', for example, offering new WHAT information in the HOW section, they will have a hard time absorbing this new information. Consider the following dialog.

Dogs are fascinating animals. They have been devoted to humankind for ages and we have learned to breed them so that we get specific physiques and temperaments from them. I think that dog shows really are beneficial because they show how our relationships with these fine animals have grown. [out of time] Oh yes, and the breeding leads us to specific behavioral tendencies. They breakup these different kinds of dogs into different categories at the dog shows. You have working dogs and sporting dogs, hunting dogs, hounds, and others. [out of time] Did I mention that there are worldwide organizations that put on these dog shows and that people come from all over? [out of time] They spend big money on grooming, training, and transporting these dogs.

It is pretty easy to see how the listener can get confused as to how to store the information they have been given. Move smoothly from the beginning to the end and reduce looping back. Phrases like, "Oh! I forgot to mention..." can confuse the listener as they try to find the right place to store this new information.

With a well-sequenced presentation, consider the amount of information you are providing at any one time. George Miller, a cognitive psychologist from Princeton wrote a paper titled, *The Magical Number Seven, Plus or Minus Two: Some Limits on Our Capacity for Processing Information.* In this paper, Miller suggests that most all people have the capacity to deal with five to nine 'chunks', or blocks, of information at one time. It is like having five to nine bins or buckets in our mind where we can hold information and we can work with these at a single time. An example of this is a phone number. Notice that when you see a phone number written like 220-809-6680. It is much easier to read and process than 2208096680. In the first case, our eyes and mind see three chunks of information made up of three or four chunks each. In the second, we perceive ten chunks of information at one time. This is much more difficult to process for the mind.

When too much information is delivered at one time, members of the audience will hit their chunking limits and will check out of your presentation until they can catch up. If it is a smaller audience that is engaging with you, they will stop you and ask you to go back and review some of the new information. This is an indicator that you are pushing a lot of information quickly.

The information in your presentation should build up in layers so as to not overwhelm the audience with too much delivered too quickly. A good rule of thumb is to deliver no more than 3 to 5 new ideas or bits of information at a time. Let the audience incorporate this new information in their understanding then add more. This will ensure that everyone in the audience will be actively listening and storing the information you are presenting.

The Satir Archetypes

Recall from Mehrabian in Chapter 3 that body language accounts for 55% of the communication of feelings and meaning. That means that even when your words and tonality are a match, if the body communicates something else, the communication you are attempting is going to be perceived, at best, as sarcasm.

Even without use of your voice, your body physiology is communicating. Let's look at how to make the most of that.

Dr. Virginia Satir, a renowned psychologist in family therapy noticed that people will embody and act out several different archetypes in a family or group dynamic. These archetypes also carry with them an associated physiology that invoke the architype response in others. Satir's five archetypes are: The Leveler, The Blamer, The Computer, The Placator, and The Distractor. In your presentation delivery, you can use each of these archetypes to evoke certain archetypical responses from the listeners.

The Leveler

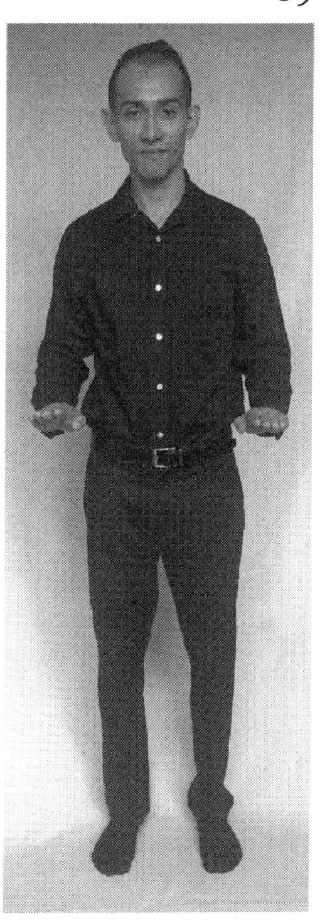

In group dynamics, The Leveler, is the clear-minded individual that sees things as they are, and he communicates very plainly with a matter-of-fact attitude. There is little emotion with The Leveler. If you could write a credo for The Leveler it would be, “It is what it is.”

The architype response to The Leveler is that this person has something very concrete to share and they are to be taken seriously. We do not expect to hear trivial facts from The Leveler, rather, their word can be trusted.

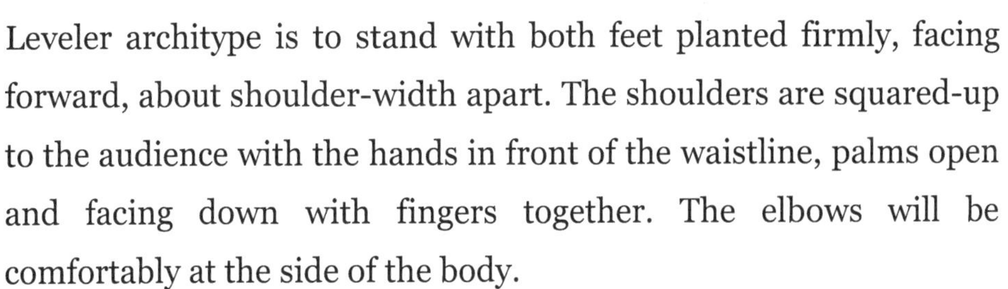

The body posture used to evoke The Leveler architype is to stand with both feet planted firmly, facing forward, about shoulder-width apart. The shoulders are squared-up to the audience with the hands in front of the waistline, palms open and facing down with fingers together. The elbows will be comfortably at the side of the body.

As you can see, the physiology is very symmetrical and stable. It also gives the appearance of strength.

Use The Leveler when you are being the expert who is communicating factual information that is above debate. Another great use for The Leveler is when you have to deliver bad news or give some very direct feedback for improvement to someone. Remember, The Leveler is a very serious person.

The Blamer

In group dynamics, The Blamer is a harsh tormenter. They will overpower others with their voice and their body posture. The Blamer is often a bully and will seek to belittle others. The Blamer commands a lot of attention.

On a positive note, The Blamer is also good at motivating people to do *something* albeit it may be motivating out of fear. In order to motivate people, you need a lot of energy and fear carries a lot of energy with it.

As an excellent presenter, you too can evoke The Blamer to get your audience moving into action.

Though The Blamer is usually perceived in a negative light, you can use The Blamer in a positive way. As a negative architype, The Blamer has one foot forward of the other, one hand clenched in a fist at his side, and the other hand at or above head-level with an accusing finger pointing at his target of blame.

To evoke this as a positive architype for a call to action, place one foot forward of the other with your weight on the forward foot. Allow one hand to hang loosely open at your side with the elbow slightly bent, and the other at the level of the head with the palm open facing in, fingers together and forward.

Use The Blamer when you have a call to action or anytime you want to ramp up the energy in your audience and to get them moving.

The Computer

Satir saw The Computer architype play out in the group as the aloof person who remained unattached to emotion or outcome. They would give the appearance that they have studied all the consequences and would be equally unimpressed with any option that was chosen; win, lose, or draw. The Computer is often like a college professor who had nothing to lose by your failure because they had all the answers and you were just not clever enough to learn what you needed to be successful. Most importantly, The Computer conveys that they have already considered all the data.

In presentations, we evoke The Computer architype as one who has given learned or considered thought to a subject. It is an excellent physiology to use when listening to questions and considering the answer. When used, it lets the audience know you have taken them seriously and have given due consideration to an appropriate response.

The physiology of The Computer is stable and well-grounded like The Leveler however, the arms are crossed with one hand positioned just under the chin.

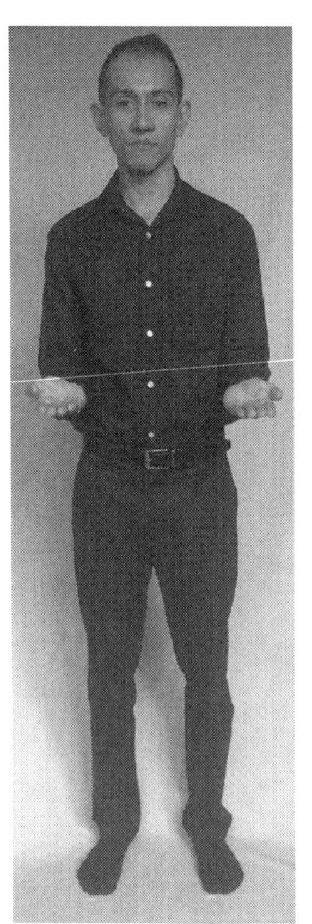

Notice here that the chin is not resting on the hand. There should not be any idiosyncratic movement of the hand or fingers. It should just remain casually under the chin while listening, contemplating, or responding to someone.

The Placator

In the group, The Placator is the submissive personality who tries to please everyone else. The Placator will self-sacrifice and allow others to be the authority over them. The Placator is subservient.

The architype response to The Placator is that he or she is weak or vulnerable. We would not see The Placator as someone who is confident therefore, over use of this architype would cause the content to suffer because The Placator would be perceived as not confident in their own abilities and knowledge.

As a presentation skill, the use of The Placator can soften the audience and evoke a sense of compassion from them. Be careful though. Unintentional use of The Placator can cause the speaker to appear weak and unsure.

The body posture of Satire's Placator is someone who is on one knee, head bowed, and arms extended forward with the palms up. As a resource in presentations, the speaker can activate this architype simply by placing both hands with the palm up. For some untrained speakers, this can be a default position for them and is one that should be identified and removed. Be conscious of your hands and only show your palms when you intend to convey a little humility.

As you can see, the physiology is also symmetrical. The hands are generally level and the palms are facing up and open.

Use The Placator when you need some forgiveness from the audience or when you need to show a little vulnerability. Imagine taking the stage to make a 45-minute presentation when the last presenter ran long and now you have 20-minutes before lunchtime. Your only option is to acknowledge the situation, change your content, and ask the audience for a little leniency. The Placator can help win the audience over to your predicament.

The Distractor

Satire's Distractor was the one in the group who tried to distract others from argument or confrontation by acting the clown or taking the conversation into a whole new direction.

The architype of The Distractor is someone who doesn't take things seriously, someone who would rather have a little fun instead of dealing with boring or controversial topics. A Distractor can also come off as passive-aggressive or mocking.

On the stage, the speaker can activate the architype of The Distractor to deal with hecklers or perhaps fix a content problem in his presentation. Once the audience is distracted, The Distractor can recapture them and redirect their attention back to the speaker and his content.

Body posture for The Distractor is very asymmetrical and may even be seen as off balance. There is no prescribe position for hands, arms, or legs. Physiologically, the key to achieve this is to appear a bit goofy.

The physiology is very asymmetrical, and the body is out of alignment and off center.

Use The Distractor as a technique to recover the attention of your audience. I once used The Distractor when I made an obvious error in my content by misstating a fact as a complete untruth. I immediately realized what I had said, as did the audience, so I smiled, got up, walked about three steps to the side, and said, "Can you believe *he* said *that*!", while pointing to the place I was standing before. I followed that with a quick shrug of the shoulders and a puzzled look on my face. Once the audience reacted with a chuckle, I walked back to the place where I had erred and continued the presentation while fixing the content error.

Using Direct and Indirect Language Patterns

Direct Language Patterns are useful for discovering new information or gathering necessary details. Direct Language Patterns ask for, or deliver, specific details in the presentation. They direct the mind to a specific mental image. "Sue is going swimming at Dustin Beach in Florida" is a pretty direct statement and leaves the listener with little need to interpret what was said.

Indirect Language Patterns are much more subtle, yet we use them constantly. Human language is full of vagueness and generalities. For no other reason than to communicate efficiently; we delete, distort, and generalize ideas and concepts in our language and leave it to the listener to determine what we meant. The listener must use context and their own attitudes and thoughts to create what they perceive as 'understanding'.

Given this dialog, "She said she was going to the coast", without perfectly accurate context we do not know who is going to the coast or even where the 'coast' is. Is the 'she' who is going to the coast the same 'she' who made the statement? We must ask, "Who specifically is going to the coast?" And, "Where specifically on the coast is 'she' going?"

Indirect Language Patterns are the opposite of Direct Language Patterns in that they intentionally create deletions, distortions, or generalizations in language requiring the listener to create meaning for himself. While this is our typical way of speaking for efficiency sake, when done purposefully, it is a powerful tool to bring an audience of many into agreement with each other and with your presentation.

Indirect Language Patterns were introduced in **Chapter One: You** as a key skill to develop. Taking the time to learn these patterns as they will allow you to have complete mastery over any conversation.

The beauty of Indirect Language Patterns is that they allow the listener to create the meaning they need. Each person makes up their own understanding of your content and they feel they have gained the information they desired.

When I first joined Toastmasters, I was encouraged to participate in a regular competition called Table Topics. In this event, one draws a topic from a hat and has two minutes to speak persuasively on the topic. I had joined a Toastmaster group that was based at a high-tech company and the topic I drew was specific to their company policies. It certainly was not something I knew anything about or could even offer any reasonable opinion. Being a willing participant, I dove into my topic with Indirect Language Patterns. As I recall it sounded something like this,

> *"The goal of business is to make money. More especially a public business like this one where each employee is duty-bound to do their best to increase shareholder value."*

> *"In order to grow the revenue of the business, we can make choices to increase sales or cut expenses. Either of these options will accomplish our goals for growth and, as we consider these two options, by far the more complex option is to cut expenses, the cost of doing business."*

"To be effective, a business must implement certain policies and the policies must be adopted by the workforce. The funny thing about people is that they will tend to do only those things that they believe are useful or create value. If the business pushed a policy into the workforce that does not increase productivity or provide some value, then the workforce will fail to adopt and implement it. Perhaps the policy will simply die a quiet death."

"As we consider the policy on <insert table topic here>, it is not for me to decide if this policy is good or bad. The employee-body will make that call and the business will adapt. One thing is certain though; a person will always do the best they can with they have been given until such time that they can change things to suit their needs."

"I do want to commend the business on stepping up. Nonetheless, if the policy is found to not achieve its intended goals, to give direction is a good thing. It helps employees band together in a common goal and achieve more than they could do individually."

"So, I ask you to consider this, how is <insert table topic here> working for you? Is this something that we, as a team will continue to support and follow or, do we, as a team, begin to chart a new direction together?"

As you read the previous dialog, it may make more or less sense depending on your setting and expectation for specific information. What it does do, quite effectively, is remain neutral without picking a side or getting into any level of specificity of details that would cause a person to have disagreement.

While I gave my two-minute presentation, I could see people engaged in what I was saying, and many would unconsciously nod their heads in agreement. What they understood me to say, or what their takeaway was... one could only guess. But they got what they wanted out of my presentation and that was my only objective.

Use Indirect Language Patterns when you want to allow the listener to create their own meaning of your language. Use Direct Language Patterns (specificity) when you want to cause the listener to think in a certain way to receive specific information. Remember, Indirect leads to agreement and Direct leads to nit-picking and disagreement.

Modulating the levels of tension (maintaining energy)

A boring presentation will be ineffective no matter the how clever or important your content. Remember that high-school teacher or college professor that droned on and on for endless hours in a monotone voice? He just did not inspire!

Modulating the levels of tension means to use your voice, tonality, and body language to create emotional states in your audience. Curiosity, wonder, happiness, joy, relief, concern, fear... are all valuable states that engage your audience to listen. You capture them into your story, and they are hooked on every word you say all the while painting those pictures in their own mind that you want them to have. This is the essence of effective and influential communication.

As you deliver your presentation, be sure you are reflecting that energy you want them to have. Use the Satir archetypes often and regularly while you modulate the tonality, speed, and volume of your voice.

The best presenters we have ever had were always great storytellers. Remember, the human mind engages in *story*. *Information* is just information but *story*, that is what activates and inspires the mind to create knowledge and wisdom.

When Multiple Presenters are Involved

When you have two or more simultaneous presenters involved, it is important to establish one presenter as the lead. This will be the person who sets the pace and advances the content. The other presenter, or presenters, should pay attention to adding additional commentary to the content enriching it with examples and alternative perspectives.

Having one person advance the content of the presentation keeps the audience together and reduces confusion in the audience.

If there are multiple presenters and each has their own content then one presenter, usually the first, should play the role of Master of Ceremonies and introduce each presenter in turn while providing a suitable segue between the presenters.

When a presenter is taking his turn, he will create rapport with all or some portion of the audience. Working together, each presenter can help the others by using a little technique called Rapport Transfer.

The technique is simple, just follow these rules:

1. Never leave the lectern or podium vacant. When introducing the next presenter, always stay and hold the space until the next presenter enters the space and receives the hand-off.

2. Always give an affirmative hand-off to the next presenter. When they enter the space, give a big smile, a nod of approval, and a great handshake, then depart with an applause for the new presenter.

Of course, there are exceptions... what if the next presenter is going to start in the back of the room? The same principle applies. Hold the space at the front of the room until the audience has fully directed their attention to the new speaker, then depart.

Answering Questions

Presentations given from a stage before an audience of hundreds or thousands usually do not have a Q&A section and, most of the presentations you will be giving day in and day out are those that engage small audiences or even a single person. In all likelihood, questions will come up. Sometimes a simple 'yes' or 'no' will suffice for answering questions and sometimes the better course of action is to find a way for the listener to create the answer they need. Stop and think about that for just a moment. Presuming you have done your job; most questions are because the listener did not fully understand your content, or they did not make that mental connection that would have otherwise answered the question.

To take your presentation skills to the next level, when a question is asked, try to determine in your own mind where the question comes from. What is it that the person asking did not understand, or what is the underlying reason for asking that particular question? With this additional information at hand, the presenter can skillfully guide the person asking to an answer that they need or perhaps add additional clarifying information. If you can help the questioner arrive at the answer their self, this is much more effective than providing an outright answer that may not have sufficient explanation for why it is the right answer.

What to do When Your Dying on the Platform

Stuff happens. Often it is unpredicted and likely out of your control. When the fecal matter impacts the rotary oscillator, you may want to run but... you can't. You are the greatest presenter these people have ever seen, and you have to own it. You have to own whatever is going on and you have to respond to whatever problems may arise.

What kind of problems you might ask? Here are some I have experienced in the middle of a presentation:

- The fire alarm goes off
- The power goes out
- The bulb in the projector dies and I don't have an extra
- An attendee passes out
- An attendee tried to discredit me
- An attendee tried to sell his product
- I got sick (like really sick)
- I said something totally incorrectly – I was wrong
- I was not prepared
- The wrong attendees showed up – no interest from them
- My 45 minutes was cut to 20 minutes
- The decision-maker got up and walked out
- And more...

Depending on the circumstance, it is possible to have the whole audience turn on you. I learned this lesson the hard way. I was teaching a class and one student, who appeared to be very needy, kept interjecting with questions that were of no value to anyone and seemed to only waste time. The first two or three times, I let them go on a bit too long telling their story. After a while, I started seeing others in the audience roll their eyes, cross their arms, lean back in their chair, and so on... eventually, because I did not handle the problem, one of the students got up and said, "I have had enough", and walked out. Another student stood up and told the person, rather directly, that they are wasting everyone else's time with their questions and that they might want to shut up. Then the whole group started to murmur in discontent. Not fun! You have to deal with people who disrupt the group, but you cannot do so too quickly, or the group will turn on you thinking you are unreasonable, too judgmental, or being too harsh. It is a fine line you must walk.

No matter the situation, the first step is to maintain control. Remember, this is your event during the time that you are the speaker. It is incumbent upon you to maintain all aspects of the situation.

If the disruption is a personal or indirect attack upon your presentation or, if you are not prepared to discuss a topic the audience is trying to drag you into, you can defer or deflect.

Deferring would sound something like this, "That is a great question/point. Give me a minute and I will get to it. We are not quite there." Or, "Thank you for raising that issue. I was not prepared to cover that during this presentation. I will get the information for you in the next day or so and send it to you."

Deflecting might sound like this, "I appreciate your comments and the main points we need to stay focused on are...." Or, "And that point is much like our topic today in which I was saying..." and segue back into your topic.

Deflection is very useful for those audience members who start to expound their story to the others in the room.

Another technique is to always have a good story. Why did they come to listen to you? What is it that they want? Remind them of this and paint the picture in their mind of that objective the way they want it. When the presentation has just gone off the rails and you need to get everyone back on track, sell the vision.

Go back to WHY. One of the benefits of 4MAT is that it helps keep the audience on track. If you are effective with 4MAT, the audience is more likely to ask the right questions at the right time. If you notice that you have not maintained 4MAT (Why, What, How, What If) and need to hit the reset button, do it. Just start over and get everybody back on pace with the WHY.

Use of humor can be a valuable tool especially when things are just too serious, and you need to lighten up the room a bit. The key to using humor is to make sure the humor is directed at yourself or some undeclared third-party. Be cautious when directing humor at an attendee. It could be taken as being made the object of a joke. That will make the person feel not so good about you or your presentation and others will notice that you take such liberties and will be on the defensive.

Sometimes, things have gone so far awry that any attempt to recover will seem contrived and pathetic. It may just be best to take your lumps and get out as quickly and gracefully as possible. In my case, I had planned an all-day meeting with a Senior Vice President and his direct reports. I had 8 people in the room whose combined yearly salary was more $3.5 million dollars. It was a powerhouse group. When it came time to start the presentation, I thanked them for coming and I began to layout the business case. I had charts, diagrams, financial studies, and a killer ROI. After about fifteen minutes the head of the group put up his hand and stopped me. “When are you going to show us the demo?”, he asked. “Uh...”, was probably the first thing that I uttered, then I told him, “I wasn’t prepared to show you a demo today.” It was at that point he closed his notebook and stared at me.

There is nothing to do in that situation except apologize, thank them for make the effort to be there, and get out as quick as possible with a promise to remedy the situation.

Set the follow-up

Depending on the type of presentation you are doing; an introduction, a training, a sales pitch, whatever... there may need to be a follow-up. If that is the case, make sure your final act is to get the next step. It keeps the momentum going. It tells you what to do next. It tells the audience what to do next. It establishes an ongoing relationship.

Finish: Chapter 7

Completing Your Presentation

If you want to build a ship, don't drum up people to collect wood and don't assign them tasks and work, but rather teach them to long for the endless immensity of the sea.

Antoine de Saint-Exupery

Wrapping Up

Completing your presentation is just as important as how you start it and you are not fully complete until you have exited the room and even perhaps, left the premises. How you leave your audience feeling will determine their lasting memory of you. It isn't what you said. It isn't what you showed them. It is always, how you made them feel. Since that is the case, it's probably worth your time to decide beforehand just what feeling you want to leave them with.

Perhaps using a closing story that parallels the success you want them to have would be a good idea. If you opened your presentation with a story, it may be useful to bring that story to a full completion; bookending your presentation. Remember, fill them with feelings.

There are some 'do' and 'do not' things to keep in mind.

First, DO NOT thank your audience for being there unless you give them a reason you are thankful. To do otherwise seems like pandering. You are the one who did the work.

Especially after a business presentation, DO NOT ask, "So what do you think?" That is just asking for objections and complaints. Instead, tell them what to do. Direct their mind to the things you want them to think. "I'd like you to consider how useful this will be in accomplishing your goals."

Now for some things to do... DO thank your audience, if they participated or brought some value to the presentation. If they spent the time and energy, show your appreciation.

DO say, "I hope I did a good job for you." Again, this draws your attention to what you want them to focus on. This also often has the effect of getting them to affirm you did give them a good presentation, which is one of the final thoughts they are left with.

DO ask, "What is the next step?" or "Think about how you will use this in order to achieve your goals." Give them something to take the energy that they have right now and move it into a successful future for themselves.

DO have a next step in mind. Be prepared with what you want them to do next.

DO offer a double-bind in order to ensure they make a choice to do something. “Perhaps you have already seen the value in our solution, or you may wish to think about it overnight. Whichever way you do it, feel free to reach out to me with any other questions.”

DO hold onto those mental states that communicate confidence. Be proud of yourself. Be proud of your company or organization. Be proud of your product or knowledge. Walk with a little swagger in your step. You just nailed it. You are the Rockstar Presenter.

Epilogue

It is my most ardent desire that you have both enjoyed this little book and have learned some valuable skills that are sure to improve your life at home, work, and in social situations. Moreover, I hope you have become an even better listener because you have a greater understanding of the intricacies of communication.

Even though you have been communicating since long before you can remember, perhaps now, for the first time, you have the skills to communicate purposefully and professionally; skillfully navigating your audience's mind through the noise of daily life to arrive at the destination they have asked of you.

Remember to go back and re-read this book from the beginning, stopping with the introduction of each new topic and taking the time to practice and truly understand how to effectively use each new skill. A little practice will go a long way to life-long learning.

When I was learning this material for the first time, I stood there in front of a group with my hands by my side (trying to NOT use them) and looking like a penguin!

It took a few moments to realize what I was doing. I became conscious again that my objective was to learn to talk while allowing my hands to rest comfortably by my side. After a couple of times; the awkwardness fell away, my hands relaxed, and I learned how to powerfully hold the space with authority.

114
Always be in a learning mode.

BE Amazing.

Made in the
USA
Lexington, KY